Cute and Cuddly: Baby Animals

FAWNS

By Katie Kawa

Gareth Stevens
Publishing

Please visit our website, www.garethstevens.com. For a free color catalog of all our high-quality books, call toll free 1-800-542-2595 or fax 1-877-542-2596.

Library of Congress Cataloging-in-Publication Data

Kawa, Katie.
Fawns / Katie Kawa.
    p. cm. — (Cute and cuddly–baby animals)
ISBN 978-1-4339-5544-0 (pbk.)
ISBN 978-1-4339-5545-7 (6-pack)
ISBN 978-1-4339-5542-6 (library binding)
1. Fawns—Juvenile literature. I. Title.
QL737.U55K39 2011
599.65′139—dc22

                                        2010052586

First Edition

Published in 2012 by
Gareth Stevens Publishing
111 East 14th Street, Suite 349
New York, NY 10003

Copyright © 2012 Gareth Stevens Publishing

Editor: Katie Kawa
Designer: Andrea Davison-Bartolotta

Photo credits: Cover, pp. 1, 9, 11, 15, 24 (fur) Shutterstock.com; p. 5 John Foxx/Stockbyte/Thinkstock; p. 7 Jupiterimages/Photos.com/Thinkstock; pp. 13, 24 (hoof) Hemera/Thinkstock; pp. 17, 19, 21, 24 (spots) iStockphoto.com; p. 23 iStockphoto/Thinkstock.

Printed in the United States of America

CPSIA compliance information: Batch #CS11GS: For further information contact Gareth Stevens, New York, New York at 1-800-542-2595.

Contents

A fawn is a baby deer.

A mother deer is called a doe.

A doe cleans a fawn.
She licks its fur.

A fawn lives with its mother. It stays with her for one year.

Fawns have four hard feet. Each foot is called a hoof.

13

A fawn's hoof has two toes.

Fawns have white spots.
These help them hide.

Fawns hide in the grass.
They hide from people.

Fawns eat plants. They eat grasses and leaves.

21

A fawn moves its ears. This helps it hear things far away.

23

Words to Know

fur

hoof

spots

Index

24